*Our lives begin in the moment
we decide to see them for the
miraculous manifestation
that they truly are.*

Copyright © 2020 Amber Lilyestrom

First published in Australia in 2020 An imprint of KMD Books www.kmdbooks.com

All rights reserved. No part of this book may be used or reproduced by any means, graphic, electronic, or mechanical, including photocopying, recording, taping or by any information storage retrieval system without the written permission of the copyright owner except in the case of brief quotations embodied in critical articles and reviews.

Cover design: Cassandra Neece

Interior design: Cassandra Neece

National Library of Australia Cataloguing-in-Publication data: Master Your Money Mind/Amber Lilyestrom XXX

ISBN: 978-0-6450371-5-9 (sc)

ISBN: 978-0-6450371-6-6 (e)

MASTER YOUR MONEY MIND

Expanded Edition

Amber Lilyestrom

To each of us who is committed to rewriting our money story,
reclaiming the truth of ourselves and living
a wildly abundant life.

xo

amber

Table of Contents

Foreword
by Rosemary Robertson Bredeson
11

Your Prosperity Perspective
13

Chapter 1
The Big Vision – What Do You Really Want?
18

Chapter 2
Your Money Memory Lane
28

Chapter 3
It's Time to Get Real About Money
38

Chapter 4
The Habit Holding Us Hostage
44

Chapter 5
The Wisdom in our Words
52

Chapter 6
Trade Competition for Creation
61

Chapter 7
Plug into Your Purpose
68

Chapter 8
The Power of Present Action
73

Chapter 9
Be a Money Magnet
80

Chapter 10
Energy is Everything
87

Master Your Money Mind for Life
93

Gratitude and Support
98

Acknowledgements
100

About the Author
102

Foreword

If you have picked up this book (or are considering reading it), you are resonating on a frequency that matches what Amber Lilyestrom is offering in *Master Your Money Mind*. Keep reading.

This book isn't one of those "Do these 5 things and you'll be a millionaire" kind of books. What it does, however, is hold your hand on a journey through a wonder-full land where you get to explore your relationship to the energy we call money. Around every corner there is something new to discover – about yourself, your history, your current story, and how you can craft a future based on your desires, not your past circumstances.

Lay aside your expectations of being told what to do, instead, reach out your hand to Amber's and let her lead you through a process that will unveil the wonders of creating a life you might only have dreamed of without expecting ever to achieve it.

We are souls incarnated on Earth to learn how to live on this planet. In the 21st Century we are dealing with an energy exchange we have labeled "money." What you can experience in this book is a deeper understanding of the lessons your lifetime is gifting you by way of prosperity and true abundance.

Take Amber's hand. Enjoy the exploration. What you will discover will change your life.

Blessings,
Rosemary Robertson Bredeson
The Scientific Mystic

Your Prosperity Perspective

Money.

There is hardly a word more charged with emotion and complexity than this one.

As I sit here writing on a Saturday morning, it strikes me that the main road across the lake is sparse with cars, a stark contrast to the scene Monday through Friday.

It's a different kind of energy, a more relaxed pace with a feeling of ease wrapped around it. People are on the road, but their intentions are different, their pace and their perspectives seem lighter.

I want to ask the people in those Monday cars, "Are you happy with where you're going? Would you rather be somewhere else?"

I remember those early mornings well. . . the rushing out the door, coffee in hand, baby being wrestled into the car seat, quick kisses and the rapid drop-off for the day of meetings, emails and full throttle living that went with it.

When our girl was three and a half months old, I began a

new version of full throttle living.

I had been on the roller coaster that was a 10-year corporate career in collegiate athletics complete with the late nights and weekends, long hours and an unparalleled devotion to my work that came with it.

I loved to teach and serve and create experiences that entertained crowds and evoked the energy that our student-athletes deserved to play in front of.

It was thrilling and fulfilling and brought me so much joy, until I experienced an awakening that would change the course of my life forever.

On the day our daughter was born, I stopped breathing on the operating room table.

After an arduous pregnancy, complete with a period of modified bed rest due to my overactivity (code for doing as a coping mechanism for my anxiety), this was my wake-up call.

Up until that point, I lived my life in full sprint mode. I didn't know any other way.

And there I was, lying on an operating room table, strapped down as my ability to breathe on my own began to fade and within moments, I was unconscious.

In that space between motherhood and this near-death doorway, I was met with a deep burning sensation of regret and rage in my core.

This surge of frustration ran deep and reminded me that I wasn't living the vision for my life I wanted most.

Now, on this most treasured day, there was a chance I

wouldn't live to meet our sweet girl.

By the grace of God, somewhere in the space between, the rage began to loosen its grip and an overwhelming sense of peace and love wrapped around me.

I saw visions of my parents, taking turns pacing in the waiting room.

I saw my husband in his scrubs, reviewing the settings on the camera one last time, waiting for the nurse to come get him to join us in the OR.

I saw myself... strapped down to the table as life was happening to me and there was nothing I could do to catch my breath and fully live.

In that split second, a massive shift happened within me... a quantum leap of consciousness took place.

This experience wasn't happening to me, it was happening *for me*.

This was the awakening my life had been leading me to.

And right there in that operating room, I surrendered... to love, to gratitude, to the appreciation I felt deep down in my bones for all of the life that I had lived, the people I had loved, the sweet little soul my body was about to bring forth.

It was a feeling of divine intervention and grace I'm not certain I'll ever be able to put words to. But on the other side of that moment, I was reunited with my breath.

It was as if the weight was instantaneously lifted and I was back... fully present for the unfolding in that moment.

And our girl was born.

Her scream was one of the most joyous sounds I've ever heard. I counted her fingers and toes over and over and marveled at her full head of dark hair and sweet face that I would soon memorize for all eternity.

The nurse ran to get Ben and we were a family.

And the truth is, I felt as if I had been reborn right there on that operating room table right alongside our girl.

On the other side, I knew that life was different now though I wouldn't find the words to express what I had experienced for months after it happened.

I knew I couldn't go back to living the way I had before. I knew that it was time to exhale and find another way to do this precious life of mine. I knew that living my life paycheck to paycheck, sprinting full tilt with no opportunity to earn a penny more was not how I was supposed to be doing my life.

I was ready to completely transform everything I had ever learned about money and the mindset required to shift the trajectory of my money story from that moment forward.

And chances are, you're in a similar position, minus the dramatic operating room story.

Maybe you're at your breaking point in your career and know there has to be something more, but you're providing for your family and that income is a non-negotiable right now.

Maybe you've launched your own business but are working tirelessly to make ends meet and still find yourself coming up short.

Maybe you're straight up exhausted and tired of money being the puppeteer controlling your life, career, emotions and relationships.

If any of this resonates, you are in the right place.

The mission of *Master Your Money Mind* is to help you reframe and completely transform your mindset as it relates to money and the abundance that is possible for your life, starting right now.
This book will take you on a journey of introspection, exercises and deep processing to help you peel back the onion of your prosperity perspective so you can set yourself free from the drama and dialogue that has been keeping you stuck.

The goal?

- Fulfillment. Joy. Presence.
- To remind you that you have everything you need and an endless supply on the way to you through the glorious gift of your existence.
- To help you recognize that your inherent state is abundance.
- To show you *exactly* how to flip the script on your scarcity story to start experiencing your life through a whole new lens.
- To open your eyes and help you tap into the stream of true and lasting prosperity that is available to us all.

Are you ready?

I am so happy you are here. I am honored to walk with you.

xo
amber

Chapter 1

Your Big Vision – What Do You Really Want?

Okay, it's time to get real.

In order to take your life and capacity to receive to the next level, we need to get really honest about what's working and what's not.

We also have to be brave enough to admit what it is that we WANT and have the courage to call it out though it's not here for us to touch and hold, yet.

The best things in life are as fun to dream about as they are to experience, and this is where we must begin.

Let's start here:

What do you want your life to look like?

What do you want to feel like when you wake up in the morning? When you login to your bank account? When you plan your family vacations? When the check comes at the restaurant? When you get dressed for the day?

What do you want to feel like in every aspect of your life?

When I asked myself this question after our daughter was born, the answer was one simple word: PRESENT.

I wanted to be present for the life I was living and for the people I was living it with.

My job had me on a daily treadmill. Every morning felt the same with a schedule I had to maintain in order to keep it all together. I felt like I was always leaving, like I could never really relax and take in the life I had worked so hard to create. I spent little time in the home I was paying a mortgage on each month and with the family I had dreamt of all of my days.

I wanted to feel abundant enough to leave that corporate career and run my own company.

I wanted to do fulfilling work that created lots of space for me to be the mama of a young babe and a creative with a big vision for her work. I wanted to get rid of the ball and chain that was our debt.

I wanted to know a totally different way of living.

But the problem was, when I wrote those words on the page, it reminded me of how far I was from that dream. Because the hard truth was, the moment my 20 to 30-minute morning journal window (if I even got to it) was up, I was off to the races to get dressed, "make-upped", and nourished – now with a baby to do the same for – all before I had to be in a staff meeting on campus.

I was living inside a chaotic rhythm that was eating me alive. And with my newfound awareness after the operating room experience, I was more miserable than ever.

I believe that once we know what it is we are here to do and how we are meant to do it, there is nothing that can erase that knowing.

That's when I turned to those who had gone before me in the quiet moments I had before bed and on my drive to work. I tuned in to those who had reached levels of success I desired. I started reading and listening to audiobooks. I tore through *The Secret, Think and Grow Rich, The Millionaire Messenger,* As *a Man Thinketh, Sacred Success, E2* and any book anyone recommended to me that had to do with money mindset and shifting my way of doing life.

Ben and I started our (tiny) debt snowball and started working as a team on our finances. We made a plan that would pay off our debt in the next 15 years, which at the time, felt impossible to commit to, but knowing that bit by bit, we were moving in the direction of our dreams gave me hope that one day things would be dramatically different.

The thing about change is that it often doesn't come in the form of a lightning bolt or even a near-death experience.

It's often found in the whispers in between the moments, in those spaces when we are faced with the opportunity to make a choice... to think differently by degrees and subtly change the course of history on our lives, often without even realizing it.

I've learned that when we attune our focus on a different frequency, we start to hear different information. When we open our minds and our receivers to new information and new ways of listening, our world begins to transform.

**In reading this book,
you are tuning into a different frequency
rightthissecond.**

You are opening your mind and your heart to consider a new way of being as it relates to money and a lot more.

When I began to really focus on my money mindset, there was something I quickly began to learn that shook me to my core.

As things began to change for me and my bank account, I realized that my struggle had nothing to do with money, at all.

Money had become the safe harbor I was hiding out in.

You see, I had known that I wanted to write books and speak on stages and share what I've learned on this life journey for as long as I can remember. It was one of my oldest dreams second only to becoming a mom.

Money had become my #1 excuse for why I couldn't go for my big dreams.

My dysfunctional relationship with money was keeping me "safe" from daring to do the things that I wanted most of all.

The amount of money in the bank had become my excuse for why I couldn't go bigger in my life.

And if I'm being honest, I was using it as a pawn in the life-long battle of unworthiness I had waged against myself.

It was easy to say, "We can't afford that" or "I don't have the time to do that, I have to work (to make the money to survive)."

I was using money as the scapegoat for keeping me small and stagnant.

Until I slowly began to learn that it was never about money at all.

So, I pass the ball to you, what if the reason you're stuck and dissatisfied had nothing to do with money, after all?

What if it was actually due to the reasons you have been allowing to keep you from the life you want to be living?

Would you say that money is at the top of that list of reasons?
The truth is the value system so many of us have been building our lives upon sits on a foundation of fear and scarcity. You can switch on the nightly news for proof.

One of the chief reasons we struggle with money is because we strive to feel SAFE, since so many of us have lived our lives feeling wounded, abandoned, devalued and unimportant.

Most of us were raised to believe that money was the panacea for our pain, and we go on striving our way through life waiting for happiness and that elusive experience of safety we're all craving.

But we can't know what true happiness and rock-solid rooting into how abundant we already are feels like if we're not willing to contemplate these concepts.

We cannot get to where it is we were born to go if we're not willing to make the sacred leaps that will lead us to more of what we desire.

Consider those Monday cars we mentioned earlier.

How many people do you know in your life who are begrudgingly driving to work (or logging on to their work computers from home – *hello 2020*), creating traffic, beeping at each other, "zombie-ing" their way to their desk?

I wonder how much those individuals value the security that money provides over their own real and lasting happiness.

I was one of them too and I lived for years believing that was how things had to be.

We have bought into the "box life" as Tony Robbins calls it.

Buy a box to live in, drive a box to a box, sit at a box all day, work on a box-shaped device, take breaks scrolling through a smaller box, drive home, eat from a box and sit in front of another box until it's time to go to sleep on a box. We have signed up for a life that is contrary to the natural design of what it means to be here and human.

Think about a child in your life.

From the moment their feet hit the floor in the morning, their imaginations are ignited.

Our daughter wakes up happy and excited for the smallest things. . . a pancake. . . her favorite doll. . . the squirrel outside on the tree.

She's excited to be awake and alive.

She, like all children who haven't been conditioned otherwise yet, only see the world through a lens of abundance. An acorn is a treasured gift the same way the toy she got on her birthday is.

She has yet to question and pick apart the parts of herself that the world has led her to believe are broken or wrong.

How could your life transform if you used a new lens through which to see it starting today?

What if this book is coming at the exact moment in time when you are ready to do your life differently?

What if this is the divine invitation you've been waiting for to zoom out on the WHOLE of your life to evaluate what's working, what's not, and where to begin with your own personal transformation?

What if it was never *actually* about the money, after all?

Chapter 1 Money Mind Journal Exercises

Grab a journal or use the space below to jot down your answers to the following questions.

- What do I truly want for my life?

◊ How do I want to feel each morning when my feet hit the floor?

◊ How do I want to serve and earn? Give and receive? Live and love?

◊ What would happen if I were able to make this mental and monetary shift in my life?

Ground into the good feelings of what you've written on the page and read on. Notice what happens as you go on with your day and think back to the good energy you ignited as you wrote these words and try to reengage with that state.

Anytime doubt or worry rises up within you, release it like a balloon string. Let it float away and remind yourself that you are in progress. This work will take time, but awareness and conscious release are two huge steps in the process.

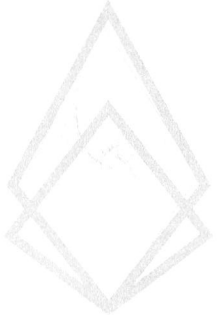

Chapter 2

Your Money Memory Lane

The truth is, we don't come into life with dysfunctional money stories. Those stories develop over time as they are influenced by the adults in our lives. And their money stories were adapted and developed as a result of what they learned from the adults who raised them.

In this case, I think about my grandfather, Herbert, who came to the United States from Germany when he was twelve years old. He didn't speak English, came from a small village in Germany and had to start his life over in a new country.

I think about my grandmother, Jessie, who came over on a boat from Scotland as a girl. Later, she raised her three children, one of whom who had cerebral palsy, and worked nights rolling needles at a factory to help make ends meet.

The time in which our grandparents lived was a different world than our modern society here today. They were born during the Great Depression of the 1920s. Struggle was their reality and money was at the center.

What's important to note is that not only were the stories of that struggle passed on to us, so were the energetics that came with it.

And the worst part? Though we live in vastly different times, most of us have carried forth the same legacy of struggle and strife even when our physical circumstances are vastly different.

When we look at our lives and our past through this lens, it's difficult to divorce ourselves of it, isn't it?

But there's another way to interpret this story.

Our grandparents overcame what would be unthinkable for our generation. I am writing portions of this book on an airplane flying in the sky on wireless internet.

Our parents were raised by parents who were products of the Great Depression here in the US and with them, they carried their own painful money stories to match. For many of us, our grandparents and great grandparents were immigrants.

I often remind myself that my grandfather and grandmother traveled to the United States via BOAT. They crossed the Atlantic Ocean by boat. When I am losing perspective, I come back to this truth and celebrate how sacred their devotion to creating a different reality for the grandbabies they would never know is to us all.

In this chapter, we will dig into the stories of your ancestors to reveal the places where you are perpetuating history that is ready to stay where it belongs. . . in the past.

Here's the reality: we are not living in a Great Depression. We are living in the most abundant time in all of history. We are living in a moment of the greatest opportunity there has ever been, no matter when you have chosen to pick up this book.

Your greatest opportunity is right now.

When we learn how to connect the dots on our own money stories and the places where scarcity reigns supreme, we can begin to unravel the places we find ourselves stuck and scared.

Your Money Memory Lane

Let's take a walk down your money memory lane.

Grab your journal and get ready to jot down a bit about your own money story.

One of my favorite ways to help people unravel their past is to simply ask them to plot it out.

To look at what's there, to do so with compassion and a greater understanding of the patterns that have been perpetuated and why, so they can release the pieces of the puzzle that no longer fit.

We cannot move forward without, first, understanding where we've been.

Turn your journal sideways and draw a line from one side of the page to the other at about the midpoint of that page (or head over to amberlilyestrom.com/moneymind to print out the worksheet).

It should look something like this:

BIRTH ——————————————————— **TODAY**

Write BIRTH on the far-left side of the line and TODAY on the far-right side of the line.

Move along the line plotting out impactful stories, memories and moments that came up in your life that served as markers for what you believe about money today.

These stories should be whatever comes up for you, positive or negative, to help mold your foundational relationship with money.

Examples might include traumatic experiences like losing a family member, a parent losing a job, your family losing your home or any significant, memorable, painful memory about money that made an imprint on you.

They might also include positive moments and memories like when you received your first allowance or bought your first house or got a holiday bonus check that made a huge impact on your life.

These stories are extremely individual so please don't judge yourself for whatever comes up. Whatever left an imprint on you and has affected how you feel about money today matters. Be sure to jot it down on the timeline.

It's also okay if you can't exactly remember when something happened. Put it in the vicinity of the time in your life when you remember experiencing it.

In this process, focus on the patterns that are coming up and how they make you feel about your life, most especially, how do they make you feel about yourself and your own worthiness?

How have those stories and patterns made you feel about what's possible for you and your life?

Are there places where a figure in your life, perhaps a parent, grandparent or major influencer on your journey, had strong opinions/beliefs about money that you have adopted too?

Take some time to sit with yourself and identify the key themes and how they relate, specifically, to the story you're living today.

When I did this exercise for the first time, I was transported back to a moment when I was about seven or eight years old. I had been watching a Lifetime movie with my mom about a little girl and her mother who were homeless. This movie must have made a significant imprint on me because a few days later, my father came home in the middle of the afternoon.

I can remember my mother's reaction and the fear in her voice when she said, "What are you doing home?"

My father holding his briefcase with his white button-down shirt and loosened tie, sleeves rolled up, shrugged his shoulders and said, "They let me go. There were layoffs at work today and I was one of them."

I watched my mother sink back into the couch, hand on her forehead, eyes closed.

I watched my dad hurriedly hanging up his coat and putting his things away.

No one said anything, but the silence was deafening.

I walked to the window, pushed the velvet curtain aside and tucked myself inside.

I looked down to the street to the corner, that looked like the one in the movie about the homeless mother and her daughter and felt the tears welling up.

Images of living in a cardboard box flashed through my mind and the central question, "Will I be able to bring Cougar (our kitten) with us?"

Hearing my dad say he'd lost his job meant in my little kid mind, that we, too, were going to be homeless like the girl and the mother in the movie.

This story, though seemingly innocuous in the moment left an imprint on me that has lasted a lifetime. I never said anything to my parents. I hid my tears and my fears away yet carried it forward.

We were raised not to talk about money. It was considered impolite. I have no idea how much money my parents earned in their careers or what they make today. This is not uncommon.

I have come to realize after coaching thousands of people in money mindset work, that treating it like a big secret only creates confusion and shame.

I can remember a moment a year or so into my entrepreneurial career standing in my master bedroom of our new home after another marathon day of baby raising and accomplishing as many tasks as humanly possible like the room was spinning.

I was way beyond overwhelmed.

Ben was in a full-time police career that he didn't love.

I had vowed that when I left my corporate career to launch my business, we would find a way to retire Ben from his law enforcement career.

I desperately wanted to create a life where we got to be

more together than we were apart.

My steady paycheck was now replaced with exponential possibilities and we had already begun to see the fruits of my labor paying off, but with it came enormous pressure to perform.

Our financial situation had already dramatically transformed from when I was in my corporate career, but the feelings that lived underneath my relationship with money had not changed.

I was still using it as a weapon in the ongoing battle I waged against myself.

Money was still a mechanism for me to measure my worth.

I've worked with countless individuals who are also living their life by this grand equation.
It goes something like this:

The more money I make = the more joy I am allowed to experience in my life.

This is what I like to call our **prosperity patterning.**

Because of lived experiences, we carry forth the notion and belief that this is how life is. It's normal and expected, therefore we don't do much to try to change it.

It's like we're waiting for the gun to go off on the start line of our lives and until we hit that magic number in the sky, we sit poised and ready waiting for someone else to pull the trigger.

We perpetuate the painful history of our past, instead of rewriting the future we're ready to live.

And instead of looking to others, outside of our direct circles, as inspiration for what's possible, we remain focused on the worst-case scenarios and the patterns of suffering and scarcity we've come to know so well.

Many spend every day of their life here and it's one of the greatest tragedies there is.

When we can embrace the reality that money is simply a tool to help us more fully express ourselves, touch the lives of others and GROW, we can change the course of history for ourselves and our families in the process.

Chapter 2 Money Mind Journal Exercises

Grab a journal or use the space below to jot down your answers to the following questions.

- ◊ What did the Money Memory Lane exercise reveal to you about your prosperity patterns?

- ◊ What insights felt like a lightning bolt of clarity?

◊ What money mindset frameworks have you adopted from well-intentioned people in your life that you're now ready to reframe and release?

◊ Whose story are you still living? What would happen if you began to live your own?

Chapter 3

It's Time to Get Real About Money

I've learned the only way to change something that's not working is to get it out into the open so things can get real.

We can't change the course of where we're going if we don't stop to plug in the right destination on our internal GPS system.

So, let's be honest together, shall we? Ask yourself:

Would you still be doing what you're doing if you knew you were going to die sometime in the next six months from today?

Would you still get in the car and go to that job?

Would you sit at that desk, wear those clothes, go to those meetings and put on the smile knowing what you knew about the time you had left?

Would you spend as much time scrolling or sipping or doing whatever it is you do to cope with the stress you feel in your everyday life?

When I went back to work after my three-and-a-half-month maternity leave, weeks after literally almost dying on the operating room table, I felt like an alien at my desk.

Everything had changed inside of me and I couldn't pretend that this was where I wanted to be any longer. I was desperately needed elsewhere.

My life was ringing me up. And the call of my soul wasn't whispering anymore, it was screaming at me every day I walked through that tunnel, up those stairs and through those doors.

I knew that the work I was now supposed to be doing in my life was outside the confines of the safety net of what I had known, and it was time for me to make a dramatic change.

Asking myself that central question was not only sobering, but wildly motivating.

And the best part?

It has led me to now living and working from our dream home here on the pond, waking up each morning to a schedule I've consciously crafted to spend my days with the people I love the most and doing work that challenges and fulfills me.

I have space for travel with my family, for creating experiences that I will take with me for the rest of my life, like flying my mom down for a week in Florida to go to Disneyworld with her four-year-old granddaughter. A moment in time we can never get back but will always remember and treasure and talk about until the day we die.

Reframing our Money Mind requires us to think differently about our lives and our time, the greatest currency there is. With this perspective shift, everything begins to change and that which felt impossible, suddenly becomes the only way forward.

Money is a catalyst for change and a resource that makes things possible, but it doesn't arrive without our enjoyment and appreciation of it.

Chapter 3 Money Mind Journal Exercises

Grab a journal or use the space below to jot down your answers to the following questions.

◊ What if you had six months to live this life, starting now?

◊ What would you do? Where would you go? Who would you need to see?

- What story would you want to leave with this world?

- What experiences would you want to make sure you had?

◊ What would you want to make sure the people you love knew about how you felt about them?

My prayer is that you will never have to live your life from a place of reaction like this, rather you give yourself the invitation to reframe and revise your sacred path right here and now.

Chapter 4

The Habit Holding Us Hostage

As a society, we have a negative thinking habit that is holding us and our big dreams hostage.

Flip on the news and watch the somber faces of the news anchors as they recant the day's troubles over and over again at the top of each hour until dinner time.

The worst part?

> ***The news streams in problem after problem and never, ever provides a solution!***

Talk about a self-perpetuating prophecy.

And yet, we plug into this thinking day after day, night after night, on the way to the office in the morning and then again at the water cooler or on our zoom chats or social media feeds.

Our set point as a society is negativity.

We would never want to get too positive for fear of looking silly when we fail or for fear of being judged by the other negative thinkers in our midst.

So we pre-pave our days and pad our interactions with others with a negativity lining and wonder why our dreams aren't coming to fruition.

Here's an interesting exercise for you to try:

Go to the local convenience store, post office or supermarket and ask the attendant how their day is going and wait for the answer.

I will bet that nine times out of ten the answer you will get is something along the lines of, "Oh, you know... hanging in there." or "Only five hours 'til my shift ends!" or... Insert your own experience here.

By and large, most people don't share their happy because they're so busy working to get to happy.

The "struggle" is the default mode. And when we set it to default mode, what do we get?

You guessed it... more of the same.

The old saying, "I have to see it to believe it" is one of the most telling statements there is.

Living from this frequency leaves no room for anything else.

What if I told you that this is only the way that life has gone, simply because it's the habit you've been practicing?

What if, like training for a road race, you can retrain your brain to cease negative thinking and begin LIVING plugged in to the vibration of that which you desire?

I am talking about mucho joy and abundance in all aspects of your life?
If your first reaction is, "Yah right, easy for you to say." I've got some incredible news for you! You, my dear, are *ripe and ready* to break this negative thinking habit today.

First thing's first, in order to break this negative thinking habit, we must lean into one of the most powerful forces we have access to and probably one you don't often think too much about.

I'm talking about our WILL.

According to the dictionary, *will* is defined as "control deliberately exerted to do something or to restrain one's own impulses and a deliberate or fixed desire or intention."

We must engage our will in order to shift the pattern of negative thinking.

And the reason why this is so paramount is because the bigger the "engine" we put behind a thought or belief, the more co-creative energy we are invoking to bring the desired result to life.

The thing we practice is the thing we perform.

Using our will to shift our negative thinking patterns will take commitment and focus, but just like training for that road race, the miles add up and before we know it, our training runs get easier and easier.

To begin your positive thought training process, here are a few steps to help you build your muscle and become more consistent.

- **Start with a simple morning routine:**

    Ground the Day with Gratitude: Wake up and think about the running list of all of the things you are grateful for while still lying in bed. See them in detail in your mind, feel the depth of appreciation you have for these people, things, experiences that have brought you joy and learning and imprint them in your physical body for the day ahead. Put your hand over your heart to enhance the feeling. Do this before your feet hit the floor each morning.

    Meditate to Feel Great: During your meditation time, sit quietly with yourself, let your breath bring you in to the present moment while you release the ticker tape of thoughts in your mind. Visualize yourself experiencing your big vision unfolding in the most magical way. Imagine it as if it is already done, signaling to the Universe that it is on its way to you in this moment. Feel the positive feelings of it all coming to life and in your physical body.

    Reflect and Receive: Sit with your journal and jot down what came to you in your visualization. Don't put any pressure on yourself to make it sound eloquent, simply get those words on the page to maximize the mind-body-spirit connection of using your physical body to practice the positive momentum of what you are dreaming in to.

- **Notice what thoughts come up throughout the day.** Keep a journal to denote how often you are catching yourself falling back into the negative thinking loops and be a detective to tap into what is triggering you to go there.

At first it might feel overwhelming, but don't lose heart, you are learning where these patterns are coming from and once you have this clarity, you will be able to change it.

When I first began this process, I realized that I had triggers hiding around every corner and it took patience and practice to start peeling back the layers on each one to figure out where they were rooted in order to totally shift them.

Once I realized how much better I felt in my physical body and how much better I felt about myself and the unfolding of my life in that process, the more the things I desired started to flow to me without all of the resistance I had been applying against them.

The positive energy state I was now creating in my life became my new set point.

Chapter 4 Money Mind Journal Exercises

Grab a journal or use the space below to jot down your answers to the following questions.

- What would happen if you adopted the mentality that you had to believe in order to see it?

◊ What if you made rewiring your beliefs your primary focus?

◊ What patterns have you been perpetuating since you woke up this morning?

◊ What do you want to BELIEVE in order to SEE?

Chapter 5

The Wisdom in Our Words

How many times in your life have you said the following phrases?

"We can't afford that right now."
"That's too expensive."
"It must be nice to be able to afford that."

My answer? Too many to count!

The "must be nice mentality" was one I carried around for longer than I would like to admit and until I realized that my envy was actually the thing that was keeping me separate from what I wanted in my life, the trajectory of abundance in my life stayed pretty consistent. . . consistently flat!

I didn't know how to grow my income. I didn't know how to increase my wealth, so it was easier to judge others for theirs than put in the work to change my situation.

And in total transparency, I didn't believe I was worthy of my wildest dreams. I used my words to keep myself safe from having to admit this to myself. Saying things were too expensive was a tactic that saved me from having to be honest about what I really wanted.

The Money Mind Mastery process is an inside job and noticing our words, our beliefs and our patterns is central to creating the shifts we desire.

Every one of us has a few buzzwords that come up in the way we think and speak about money. The interesting thing about our buzzwords is they reveal a deeper story beneath the surface about what we really think.

When we call something expensive, we are labeling it as something that is, actually, not a priority to us in the present moment.

Think about it, when you say something is "too expensive," you are justifying to yourself why you don't want it or can't have it right now.

We are separating ourselves from the thing we desire with our words, thus creating a conscious commentary on what we value and what we believe to be true.

Recently a potential new client said that the program price tag was "too expensive." I redirected her to stand in her power and use words that helped her claim what it was she really wanted right now.

Once she understood this concept, she agreed that what she was craving was more security, not expansion and so she was not, actually, ready to invest in her business at the present moment; however, she was grateful for this perspective shift.

Another new client had the opposite experience and never used the word "expensive" though the investment was a big leap for her. She paired it with her desire to expand

and grow her business and felt joy at the opportunity to receive what was on the other side of her enrollment in the program.

Our words are directly connected to how we feel about what it is we desire and our proximity to those things.

> **Becoming more intentional with our words is not only a game changer with our money mindsets, but with our entire lives.**

Let's play a little game to help you start consciously using your word as your wand:

Get out a pen and a piece of paper and write down three things you want right now that you may think are too "expensive" for you to own or invest in. Now... look at that list.

How do those three things make you feel when you think about them?

Close your eyes and do a body scan if you need to.

- Does it make you feel limited? Anxious? Depressed? Frustrated?
- Does it make you feel like you're never going to get to a place where spending *that* kind of money feels effortless?
- Does it make you feel further from your big dreams?

Chances are, you said "Yes" to one of those questions and rest assured, I've been there too.

The word "expensive," in and of itself, is a charged one. We hear it on social media, we hear our loved ones and our potential clients say it on a regular basis. No wonder it's so hard to shake it.

Let's break it down to help you get clear about why your Money Mind is being impacted by words like expensive.

According to the dictionary, expensive means "to cost a lot of money."

When I hear that definition, it leads me to one question: who determines what qualifies as "a lot?"

I can remember saving up my quarters to buy a package of Skittles at the convenience store for my dad's Sunday run to get the newspapers.

I would tag along in the car with a pocket FULL of coins and when I proudly put my package of candy on the counter alongside my mountain of change, there were some days that the cashier would be counting my money down to the penny because that was all I had.

I felt like I was rich and believed that a package of Skittles cost a lot of money back then.

"A lot of money" has a very different definition to a four-year-old and a forty-year-old, doesn't it?

The good news here is that the definition of the word "expensive" is completely subjective and dependent on one person. You.

When we label something as "expensive," we're simultaneously and subconsciously saying that we're separate from what we desire.

I'm willing to bet that at one time or another, you've told yourself the story that this thing; this experience, this program, coach, trip, house, car, new pair of shoes... whatever

- is outside of the limits of what you can have or ACHIEVE, thus becoming a #SelfFulfillingProphecy that dictates the trajectory of your life. . . and thus, your overall feeling of satisfaction and possibility.

Are you ready to revise that statement?

What we tend to lose sight of, however, is that when something we want is in alignment with who we are and what we need to be of greatest service to the world and to ourselves, the conditions must adjust themselves to make it possible for us to say "Yes."

Take, for example, a Mastermind coaching program I was invited to join recently.
When I saw the price tag on it, I had a little moment of doubt (Okay, more like a week's worth with lots of questions and calls to friends). I knew I had enough money to invest in the deposit. . . but, in the spirit of unabashed realness- I had no idea where the rest of it was going to come from.

I was terrified to commit because I wasn't sure how I was going to come up with the money to make it happen.

But since I knew this was THE thing to help me take my business and mindset to the next level, similar to when I walked away from my ten-year corporate career with one client on the books, I took the leap.

I sourced my past experiences to give me the fuel to say YES to where I wanted to go. I knew that the new ways of thinking I would be exposed to through learning with the great minds and souls of those in the group, would help me to source the inspiration and information I needed to create something to pay for the whole program.

It was about how I could elevate myself to a higher level

and serve my greater purpose, while simultaneously, creating more freedom for myself and for my loved ones.

It was completely aligned with the direction of where I wanted to go and when I thought about it, I felt alive inside, even though my old money mindset still created some fear for me about where I was going to find the rest of what I needed for the investment.

The bottom line was this: it was a priority. I didn't view the 5-figure investment as expensive because it was perfectly aligned with my big vision coming to life and I was just gifted an opportunity to get on the fast track.

Guess what happened next?

On the other side of my sacred YES, it no longer became an option to question where the money was going to come from.

I was now in co-creative harmony with the abundance of the Universe.

I clicked into the reality that this invitation came at a divine juncture on my journey and it was time for me to answer the call.

One week after the program started, I went to my first event with the Mastermind crew and handed over a big ol' 5-figure check for the remainder of my balance.

Cue the wonder twins: Alignment + Intention.

We are constantly robbing ourselves of the opportunity to want something that could potentially change the way we experience this life when we use a word that sets a limit on what's possible.

And we use words like "expensive" to keep us from going there and to keep us safe from disappointment.

My invitation to you is to consider your priorities, your big vision and where you want to go. Moreover, I want to invite you to watch your words like a hawk.

Our words shape our lives.

Our words gave birth to the reality we are living right now. Our words can be life-giving and hope-filled or the opposite of that. And those words are ours to choose.

Chapter 5 Money Mind Journal Exercises

Look back at that list we crafted with those 3 things you are dreaming about and yourself. Grab a journal or use the space below to jot down your answers to the following questions.

◊ Are those things what I really want or are they stepping stones to get what I really want?

◊ How could I shift my words to make room for those things starting right now?

◊ How often in my day do I use words that diminish me and my Big Vision?

◊ What would happen if I started to take ownership for consciously changing those words throughout the day?

Chapter 6

Trade Competition for Creation

One of the most common trends I see in the entrepreneurial space is people spending the majority of their time plugged into what other people are doing in order to make decisions about what's going to be most profitable, inspiring and effective in their businesses.

They are waiting for creative inspiration from thought leaders and teachers in their industries, rather than being thought leaders and visionaries themselves right now.

They spend more time scrolling through social media sites (code for comparing and judging) than they do creating their own powerful content to help improve the lives of others and themselves in the process.

Here's the truth: competition equals co-dependency.

It means that your worth is reliant upon others in order for your success to be achieved.

Competition, in and of itself, is built on the notion that

there is a limited supply available and we are in constant pursuit of that dwindling supply.

And the end result? Growth or death.

I don't know about you, but when I am living inside my business on the fear hamster wheel, nothing good comes from that place.

Creativity, on the other hand, intuits that each and every one of us has the capacity for unique and individual contribution on this planet.

Living a creative life eliminates the need for competition.

Creation builds upon the spirit of contribution, of moving the needle forward for humanity versus scratching and clawing to survive.

The moral of the story?

Get busy creating. Stop competing and watch how your life (relationships, career, business) begins to bloom.

The names of the authors, artists, athletes and amazing talents that we remember were the ones who busied themselves with their own creations and commitment to their gift above all else.

Focus your positive energy in positive work that makes space for holding the mental image of what you want to bring into being.

If you want to live a more abundant life, practice living a more abundant life now. Take present, inspired action and birth what's next.

The things we create are the things that generate the revenue, connections and relationships that LEAD to money.

Creation energy is abundant.

The most direct way to think our thought into things is to practice appreciation for those things as they are making their way to us, rather than rehearse all of the reasons they are not here yet or why they might be delayed along the trail.

My favorite way to overcome resistance with this line of thinking is to consider the experience of going to a restaurant and ordering your favorite meal.

You sit down with eager anticipation in thinking of what that dish is going to taste like, what the smell will be when it arrives, how much you will treasure and enjoy it.

The imagery is so vivid you can enjoy it as if it's already on the table in front of you while you wait.

And then, the moment it arrives, the experience is as sweet in the tasting as it was in your mind before it arrived. Not for a second did you question its arrival or the pleasure of its becoming.

But consider this...

Imagine you were frantically pacing the restaurant floor, asking every wait staff member as they left the kitchen if it was actually coming or if it was going to be good. You would be considered a crazy person for this behavior!

But when it comes to abundance, this is how so many of us behave.

Let's apply this example when we think about the promotion or the house or the car or the new clients we are so excited to work with.

Imagine if, like your favorite dish on the menu at the restaurant, you could place your order with the Universe and trust that the "waitress in the sky" is on her way to bringing it to you?

Imagine if, instead of doubting and stressing and questioning if it was going to come, you relaxed and trusted that it was on its way to you?

What if you could go on with your conversation with friends, living your life, dreaming into what's next rather than panicking and freaking out because your meal hasn't arrived yet.

How could using this analogy to think about the things you are creating and that big vision you are bringing to life in your own experience change the sacred in-between space you are in right now?

Chapter 6 Money Mind Journal Exercises

Grab a journal or use the space below to jot down your answers to the following questions.

◊   Take some time to write down what you are excited to create.

- Think about what sort of energy would help bring it into being and where you could clean it up a little bit and practice more of what we discussed in Chapter 4 with creating new habits of thinking.

- Where are you spending more time plugged into competitive thinking energy versus creative thinking energy?

◊ How could you transform your thoughts about competition with a colleague or industry peer into creative collaboration or co-creation?

◊ What if you looked at their social media profile and instead of feeling envy, you recognized that you are both putting out good in the world to help people live their best lives? How would this change the way you experience your own work?

Chapter 7

Plug into Your Purpose

I talk with entrepreneurs from all over the world every day and the one central factor that separates those who are on the pathway to massive success and those who aren't is one simple thing. . . how plugged into their purpose they are.

When there is no clear meaning or deeper purpose pulling us forward on the path, there's no point.

When we're disconnected from the WHY behind what we're doing in our lives and careers, we feel like we're on treadmill with no end in sight.

You have to know your purpose.

You have to understand **WHY** *you want money and what that money is for.*

Money is simply a tool to help us expand more fully in to our potential and in alignment with our divine purpose for being here.

Money is here to help us experience greater joy and to help others do the same.

Money is no different than your car or the Wi-Fi you use every single day, both are vehicles to help you get your message and your heart out there to lift others and lift you in the process, as well.

When was the last time you connected the dots on your bigger purpose and the way you are earning money in this moment?

Tell me, why did you take on the job you are currently working today?

Think back three, five, ten years ago and remember why you said yes to the job(s) you were working then.

Were they leading you closer to your big vision and to the purpose that lives beneath that big vision?

I can think back to my first job while I was in college. I worked at night and during school breaks as a housekeeping staff member in the Field House, the place where I was a Division I athlete at the time.

I didn't fully understand why I felt called to do that job back then, but I knew that it would get me in to the offices of the administrators of the athletic department in a more casual setting.

I would empty their trash cans and vacuum their offices and sometimes find myself sitting in the chair across the desk of one of the head coaches or the athletic director, himself, talking about my career as an athlete and what I wanted to do once I graduated.

I knew I wanted to be where the leaders were and it was

there that I got to share what lit me up and what my bigger purpose at the time was.

It's no coincidence that my first job out of college was as the Marketing Coordinator of that very athletic department.

I went from making $10 an hour to $20,000 per year, which was A LOT of money for me back then. I truly felt like I was rich.

I had a job I loved, a career I had the opportunity to grow in and a community in my place of work that knew me and believed in me as a whole person because I had spent so many hours getting to know them while working in the housekeeping department and playing soccer.

Think back over the dots of your life and look at how the puzzle pieces fit together to zero in on that bigger purpose and how it has been playing out in your life already.

The best part about being plugged into our higher purpose is that it serves as jet fuel when we get stuck and frustrated and when things don't seem to be going exactly how we want them to be.

Your purpose is what will put you back on the path when you've lost your way.

Your purpose is what pulls you toward ultimate fulfilment.

Chapter 7 Money Mind Journal Exercises

Grab a journal or use the space below to jot down your answers to the following questions.

◊ What is your deeper purpose?

◊ What lights you up?

◊ What has been calling to you for longer than you can remember?

Not sure and needing some clarity? Head over to *amberlilyestrom.com/quiz* to take the Core Purpose quiz to figure out your Core Purpose archetype.

Chapter 8

The Power of Present Action

Awakenings are a funny thing. . . they give you the clarity to recognize that it's time to make a change, but they never seem to come with a roadmap.

On the other side of that day in the operating room, I was now a new mom with a whole host of complications to deal with, a ton to learn about how to care for our new baby, a job I was on maternity leave from for the next three and a half months, a husband with a full-time police career, a mortgage to cover, a car payment, food to put on the table and all of the things that come with it.

The pressure was intense, but my maternity leave, though not a paid vacation, was the first time I had permission to step away from the machine that had become my life.

It gave me the space to start dreaming into what I wanted more of. It gave me the opportunity to experience what it would feel like to not have to get up every day at the crack of dawn to go to a job that was slowly sucking my soul out and requiring me to be someone other than who I was.

My path had led me here and it was time to start listening.

But the hard reality was, as I have shared, I had no idea where to begin.

I knew what we were making every month, I knew that there wasn't much of a cushion and even though we had started our own "debt snowball" process with paying down the bills with the highest interest to eliminate our debt, it still felt debilitating.

My salary combined with Ben's helped us make ends meet, pay our bills and have a little extra to go out to dinner a few nights per month.

And because our jobs required so much of our time, and now as new parents, there was hardly a place for growing that bottom line in the structure of our lives.

I dabbled in network marketing but couldn't get much going and though I was promoted every two years in my corporate career, it never felt like we were making any ground financially.

It felt pretty hopeless for a while, but through my newfound love of personal growth and development, I became fascinated with studying those who were doing what I wanted to do.

I can remember sending an email to Mel Robbins who was then a radio host and retired lawyer before she was the best-selling author rock star she is today saying, "I want to do what you do when I grow up. Would you be open to a 10-min informational phone interview for me to ask you a few questions?"

To my surprise and elation, she said yes, and it sparked a friendship that we still have to this day.

After learning about Mel's journey and the journey of other incredible entrepreneurs, I realized that in order to get where I wanted to go, I had to be willing to go first.

I realized that I had to take action in the NOW in order to make way for the HOW.

I knew that I wanted to be a coach. I knew that I was here to help people step into their greatness, even if I questioned if I was actually doing that. I knew that wallowing in my doubt was not helpful. I was clear that leveraging the experience and credibility I had already garnered as a branding and marketing professional was going to be my ticket.

I realized that I couldn't help someone without first becoming my own success story and so I made a commitment to myself that I would not quit on this dream, no matter how frustrating or useless it all felt at times.

I didn't have much money to throw at this new endeavor. I didn't know how to position myself, but I did know that education would be the doorway to new possibilities.

I scraped up some of our savings and joined a program and began working with a coach who generously donated her time to me (I love you Zoe!).

I can remember the moment I clicked purchase on that program. It was the MOST I had ever spent on myself at one time. My palms were sweaty, but I knew that getting this dream in motion was going to require action in the present moment to bring my dream to life.

Over to you: What are you working and waiting on?

What do you need to say YES to right now in your life to equip you with the skills and know-how required for you to grow in the direction of your dream? Get creative about what will grease the skids and serve as a creatively inspired commitment to what it is you're ready to welcome into your life.

Growth requires a commitment to consistent inspired action.

One of the most prominent challenges I see my students facing is keeping up with consistent inspired action and not getting discouraged when the results don't register on the Richter scale of what they deem as worthy.

Our thoughts are consistently creating our reality. Is it possible to break the habit of negative thinking when we don't nail the landing or hit our goals?

Your ultimate success is relying on you to repattern this part of your psyche.

Disappointment kicks off a chemical reaction in our bodies and ignites our cortisol which is our main stress-producing hormone. Doubt keeps us in hypervigilance and overthinking. We are wiring ourselves to stay stuck in frustration when we live here.

Negative thinking is, by far and away, the most destructive habit of humanity.

The addiction runs so deep it's a way of being for most, which leads to additional addictions - drugs, alcohol, overeating, cigarettes, etc. to "numb" away the intensity of what chronic negative thinking feels like in our physical bodies and emotional world.

Overcoming the negative thinking habit is possible by committing to the present moment and reframing the way in which we have been living our lives.

Make it an inspired action in the present moment. . . which

will align with our purpose and, ultimately, our power to create positive outcomes.

So what does this have to do with money?

I could not have left my steady paycheck without creating enough momentum to become the magnet for the money I was ready to welcome into my life. Keep reading to learn, exactly, how to do that.

Chapter 8 Money Mind Journal Exercises

Grab a journal or use the space below to jot down your answers to the following questions.

- ◊ What present action do you need to take today to shift your current money situation?

- ◊ What investment do you need to make in your future?

◊ What do you need to clean up, cancel and release in order to get closer to your goals?

◊ What are you going to do TODAY to create momentum towards your big vision?

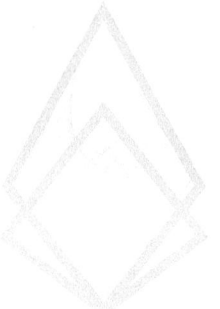

Chapter 9

Become a Money Magnet

As I mentioned in Chapter 8, I could not have changed my family's financial situation without creating momentum around the new ways of attracting abundance in our lives.

And I couldn't create those new "containers" for receiving in the way of my two businesses without taking inspired action to welcome in the clients who were ready to work with me.

I want to share with you the equation that will, literally, change the game for you when you begin to invoke it in all aspects of your life.

The only catch?

You cannot discriminate the definition of abundance as it weaves its way into your life.

I had to learn that a penny on the sidewalk or the opportunity to do a trade agreement with a colleague were both equivalent to abundance in my life even though they didn't equal the SUM of dollars I was praying for in my bank account.

When we view and receive abundance with an unconditional lens and see it as our opportunity to practice receiving, our bank accounts and the whole of our lives begin to transform.

We begin to see that flowers blooming on a sidewalk are a sign of abundance for us.

We begin to recognize that our child drawing a picture for us is abundance and a demonstration from the Universe of our unconditional ability to receive at any time.

Once we click into this realization, we begin to see everything, including the hawk flying overhead as a gift that reminds us of all that is available to us in each moment.

Once we adopt this abundant way of LIVING, it becomes impossible to operate in a place of lack and scarcity.

And since we can only contribute from our highest good when we're living in a place of true alignment with our purpose, our beliefs and our power, we will find our new set point to be that of Abundance and no longer fear and scarcity after a period of intentional practice.

I'm a practical gal, though, and at the beginning of my Money Mind journey, I found myself feeling a little skeptical of anything I perceived to be woo-worthy.

In my process of wanting to create a framework to follow in my work with entrepreneurs, I discovered an equation that has led me to building a million-dollar business that has made an impact on thousands of lives and families all over the world.

I want to share this equation with you as I know it will

change your life and become a go-to tool you lean on when you feel yourself getting swirled up and confused on where to go and what to do next in your career, your relationships, your business and beyond.

The only challenge is, you cannot skip a step in this process. Each element of this equation is required to get to the desired result.

I call it the Master Your Money Mind Equation

MISSION + MOTION + MOMENTUM + MAGNETISM = MAGIC/MIRACLES/MONEY

Let's break it down:

Mission - Our purpose, our meaning, our MISSION is what kicks off the equation. We have to know WHY we want what we want and what having that thing (whether it's the pair of shoes or the private jet) means to the bigger mission of our lives here. The good news? It doesn't require you to be a living saint, simply making your mission to live a fully present and joy-filled life is enough. And the good news? The vibration of fully present, grateful and joyful is a vibrational match for abundance.

Fact: When we are able to live a fully present life with joy as our central objective it is impossible to not make a positive impact on the lives of others in the process. Try it and see.

Motion - We cannot get from point A to point B without ACTION. You've got to get your mission in motion. Be of service, share what you've learned. Quality leads to quantity... get in motion and have fun being the creator that you were born to be. Watch what happens next.

Momentum - Sustained motion equals momentum, which requires less force and exertion over time. Momentum is the key to growing our wealth and piling on positive emotions to make way for more and more of it. Get yourself in to a state of momentum by committing to consistent (not constant) motion in service of your mission.

Magnetism - A physical phenomenon results once momentum has set in. Think about any great musician or personal brand you love. It's hard to describe what it is you love about them; you just know they keep showing up in your newsfeed (independent of the algorithm) and you love everything they are doing and saying. They have positively charged their mission to result in the magnetism that has attracted you to them. You can do this too, in your bank account, in your business, in the way you interact with others.

The end result?

Magic, Miracles, Money. . . and all of the good things you desire on the other side of your Big Vision coming to fruition.

MISSION + MOTION + MOMENTUM + MAGNETISM =
The MAGIC/MIRACLES/MONEY *you're dreaming about!*

Chapter 9 Money Mind Journal Exercises

Grab a journal or use the space below to jot down your answers to the following questions.

◊ What is your mission?

◊ What do you need to get in motion right now?

◊ What sort of momentum do you anticipate creating?

◊ What does magnetism in your life, brand, business, career mean to you?

◊ What new levels of magic, miracles and money are you ready to attract?

Chapter 10

Energy is Everything

It is no secret that our day is dictated by the energy with which we approach it.

When your feet hit the floor in the morning, what does the running tape in your head say?

What are you dreading having to do and how is that dread casting a shadow on your dreams and the way you're showing up in your life?

We cannot get into a state of attraction and inspiration. . . our creative flow. . .if our energy is blocked and drained by focusing on things that we loathe.

Enacting the principles you've learned in this book is a life and death matter.

I was living my life half-alive, and though you might not have been able to notice it from the outside, I was exhausted. And if I am being completely honest, there were days when I would drive by the hospital in our town think to myself, "I wish I could just go there for a little while and be just a little sick so I don't have to have so much pressure on me to do all of the things in my life."

This breaks my heart to admit, but I felt so hopeless at times, I didn't know any other way out than to pray for taking a break that was (seemingly) beyond my control to actually get one.

It feels awful writing those words on the page, but I had backed myself into a corner, and I felt I had no way out.

Chances are, you or someone you know, has been there too.

And in my mind, the one central thing holding me hostage was money.

I blamed it all on money.

Money was the bad guy and it was the self-proclaimed limiter of my life.

And here's the thing, I've watched countless people in my life live their lives this way too. . . up until the day they died, they believed that the only impediment to their lives being better was money.

It's tragic to think about, but this doesn't have to be your life too.

You get to decide what the trajectory of your life looks like.

And like all of the other things you've learned along the way, like how to eat healthier or be more productive in your job or how to move on from a relationship that no longer worked for you, you can do the very same with money.

This book outlines the principles to reframe and reset your

Money Mind.

It requires the radical personal responsibility to go with it.

The way you think about money, the way you practice your beliefs about money and how money shows up as a result in your life can be completely transformed by focusing on the one central factor you will be able to control for the rest of your life.

Wonderful, magical, marvelous You.

Your Money Mind emanates from your deeper sense of purpose and your mission on this planet.

It radiates outward in alignment with the vibe of how you are TRULY showing up in your life and work in the world.

Law of Attraction is based upon the notion that like attracts like.

When we line up each of these things, we can prove to ourselves that in order to get where we are going, money will be along for the ride as a tool to fuel our magnificent journey and to make an even bigger impact as we go.

Chapter 10 Money Mind Journal Exercises

Grab a journal or use the space below to jot down your answers to the following questions.

◊   My purpose for being here is…

◊ My mission for my lifetime is…

◊ Money is a tool to help me…

- Improving my Money Mind habits, and beliefs will....

- Taking present (inspired) action means, I am ready to...

Now off you go. . . get your mission in motion to create the momentum and magnetism to attract all of the tools, resources, people and magic you need to make a massive impact during your time here.

Master Your Money Mind for Life

What if we could plug in to a new way of looking at the Universe and recognize how abundant it truly is and watch our lives expand in the process?

Is your heart beating a little faster?

Are you ready to embark on this journey for the rest of your life?

The possibilities are truly endless, and I've got a little secret for you...

Those big "Beyoncé-level" dreams belong to you because they are for you.

> ***If the dream is in you, it's for you.***

Our dreams come to us because they are our soul's way of expressing itself.

Author J.K. Rowling, one of the wealthiest women in the world, was a single parent on welfare when she wrote *Harry Potter*.

She wrote on her website, "As soon as I knew what writers were, I wanted to be one. I've got the perfect temperament for a writer; perfectly happy alone in a room, making things up."

She wrote her first book at age 6 and then went on to write her series of seven books selling more than 450 million copies. J.K.'s money story was a mess, yet she kept going because she was pulled by something bigger than her fear.

For the sake of the exercises in this book and for the trajectory of your life, we have to get beyond the fear.

We have to start to learn how to trust fall with the Universe and with our sweet selves.

I know what it feels like to have a death grip on the wheel of my life.

I literally drove myself to the hospital when I was in labor because asking for help wasn't natural for me. The doctor told me to get someone to drive me, I decided not to ask my neighbor because, "it would be easier to just do it myself." I lied to the doctor and got in the car, waiting to pull out of the garage in between contractions.

Little did I know, I was headed to the hospital not only to give birth to my little girl, but to birth the next version of myself.

My life before was riddled with limitation and excuses and the notion that I was separate from the life that had been calling to me.

Wow, did I have that all wrong!

It wasn't until I learned that this wasn't an impossibility, that the dreams that had danced in my heart and soul for all the days of my life were the invitation for my creative spirit to SOAR, to make an impact, to serve, to EXPAND beyond measure.

It was not until I learned that the train tracks of suffering and scarcity were not my natural inheritance or in the best interest of the future I was born to create.

I learned that it was, in fact, my destiny to be here and to remember to remember that to be alive is a miracle in and of itself and that if I was able to love my child with the deepest sense of devotion I had ever felt in my life from the moment she got here, then why would I be worthy of any less than that, myself?

I discovered that walking the path home to myself, to my sacred work in the world - my expression for what the meaning of my life is truly about – Love - was my reason for being here.

I was gifted the realization in that operating room that when we die, all that's left is divine grace, love, reverence and appreciation.

> ***I'll never forget the beauty and wonder of what I felt there.***

And I come forth with this message for you. If, in fact, all that's there to meet us when we die is a sensation of deep appreciation and love for who we are and who we've gotten to do life with, what are we so afraid of it while we're here?

My wish for you, dear reader, is that this book awakens in you the invitation to wrap your arms around yourself, your life and the world in which you've created that belongs only to you.

My prayer is that you will see you are not alone on this

journey, rather that you have been guided here, to this specific moment in time.

You have the gift of waking up to another day. You have the blessing of getting to feel the warm sun on your face, to hear the voice of a loved one, to look into the mirror at those eyes that have been staring back at you all the days of your life and be who it is you were born to be.

What if it was never about the money, after all?

What if you could set yourself free from this equation of pain and the need to control every aspect of your life and make room for the flow that is our purest and most natural state?

What if I told you that the way you show up in your life, energetically and emotionally, is a mirror for your experience of money and the resources and relationships and all things abundant you will ever need?

What if you woke up tomorrow and decided to enact the principles of this book, the Master Your Money Mind Equation, the discoveries from your Money Memory Lane exercise and commit to your own personal evolution henceforth?

Our lives begin in the moment we decide to see them for the miraculous manifestation that they truly are.

You are rare. You are a treasure to behold.

When we take to the world with wet wings and step into our greatness, we no longer live in a state of perpetual fear, rather we enter a state of perpetual possibility.

Go, feel the wind in your hair, create magic today, gift the world your brilliance and watch what comes back to you in the process.

Open your palms and your heart and use your voice for upliftment and joy and your life will be transformed forevermore.

This is the secret to mastering your Money Mind.

Gratitude & Support

The intention of this book is to lead you home to yourself and to the reality that your money story is an inside job. We all start where we are, and we have the opportunity each and every day to move the needle forward from wherever we begin.

You do not need to be a millionaire, to own your own business or to even have a job to enact these principles and exercises to transform your life.

I urge you to read this book a few times, at different chapters on your journey as you grow and learn and expand into the fullness of who you really are.

My prayer is that this book will inspire you to see what's possible and to start taking radical personal responsibility for your life in a way that leads to unimaginable success and fulfillment.

And if you found value in what I've shared here, I would love to hear your story and how this book has impacted your life. I love to receive emails, DMs and messages from my tribe! Be sure to tag me on Facebook and Instagram: @amberlilyestrom

If you know someone who would LOVE and needs this book, send them to: MasterYourMoneyMind.com

I also host a podcast called The Amber Lilyestrom Show where I am interviewing authors, mentors, spiritual teachers, athletes and incredible guides every week. You can check it out at amberlilyestrom.com/podcast

If you would like to learn more about my upcoming programs, live events and coaching offerings, head over to amberlilyestrom.com

I look forward to connecting with you further!

xo
amber

Acknowledgements

Thank you to my beloved friend, soul sister and partner in this writing journey, Adrea Peters. You are a genius, a treasure, a gift to my life. Thank you for helping me do the thing. You give me wings.

Massive love and gratitude to the brilliant Cass – your art is a blessing, your talent unparalleled. Thank you, my dear!

Thank you, Karen, for the opportunity to be a part of your dream and the KMD Family! Boundless gratitude!

Deep appreciation to my students for your courage, your vulnerability, your hearts. This book is for you. To Melissa, Meg, Rick, Erika, the first four clients to gift me the honor of serving you and walking with you on your journeys. I will never ever forget you and the magnificence of your dreams.

To my dream team and beloved sisters, Liza, Kristen and Jamie. Thank you for inspiring me to give bigger and believe in me in ways I never knew possible. I love each of you dearly and am so thrilled we get to be framily and world shifters together.

To my dear friend Rachel Camfield. Thank you for reminding me to live in the wonder that is my life. Thank you for gifting me grace, believing in me and my work with unwavering devotion and love. Your friendship is one of the greatest gifts. How blessed are we?! I love you.

To my incredible mentor Rosemary Robertson Bredeson, your guidance and knowingness of my soul has been like Miracle Gro for my life's path. Thank you for helping me to expand beyond possibilities. I love and appreciate you!

To my friend and mentor Tim Storey, thank you for showing me the way. Thank you for leading with light and love and being exactly who you are. You are a legend.

To Mom and Dad for your persistence and passion, for the ways you have led me so well and loved me every second of my existence. Lucky ME to be yours. I love you so. xoxoxooxoxooxox

To Ben for being my partner on this journey, for walking with me through the weeds and the wonder. I am obsessed with the life we have created and the perpetual magic we get to experience here together with our sweet girl and beloved furry fam. You are my rock. Thank you for believing in my crazy ideas every step of the way.

To my darling girl, Anni. . .you are abundance embodied in flesh and bone. Never, ever forget it! You are the greatest joy I've ever known. May your life feel as magical as it has always been, from the very first beat of your bold, gorgeous heart into forever. Thank you for being the one to remind me to let it be easy over and over again. I am so happy I get to do life with you!

About Amber

Amber Lilyestrom is a transformational branding strategist and business coach, author and speaker. Her work has been featured by *Forbes*, *Entrepreneur* and *Working Mother Magazine* and appeared on countless top-rated podcasts.

Amber helps visionary entrepreneurs and CEOs align their purpose with their profit and position themselves as sought-after experts and thought leaders through her life-changing Brand Love Method™.

She is the author of multiple books, including *Paddle Home*, *Master Your Money Mind* and co-author of *Quantum Wealth*. Amber lives on a lake in the woods of New Hampshire with her husband Ben and their daughter Annika.

Let's connect on Instagram @amberlilyestrom or over at amberlilyestrom.com

Other Titles by Amber Lilyestrom

Paddle Home: Surrendering to the Stream of Our True Being

www.ingramcontent.com/pod-product-compliance
Lightning Source LLC
Chambersburg PA
CBHW021957290426
44108CB00012B/1109